HOW TO MAKE THE GREATEST PIZZA ON EARTH

By Jim Neidert

Edited by Sara T. Bredesen

Jim Neidert

Visit my website at https://www.homepizzaparlor.com/

Printed in the United States of America

First Printing: May 20, 2020

ISBN: 9781728760988

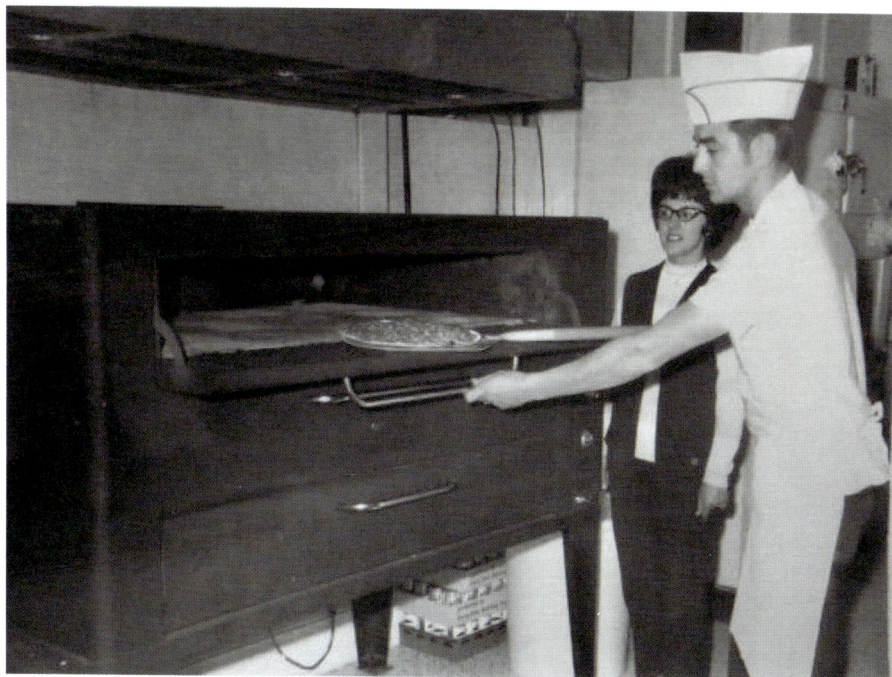

Jim and Sherry Neidert operated "The Pizza Corner," 1971.

FOREWORD

I was introduced to pizza in 1958 when I was 14 years old. Pizza was just coming on the scene in the United States. That's when Pizza Hut started, along with three of my other favorite-to-be pizza places. Pizza became an obsession. I ate it seven nights a week and tried to get into every commercial pizza kitchen I could in order to learn the art of making this fabulous food.

Although no one shares their "secret" formulas, it became my quest to make the world's best pizza. I observed it all—from fresh, to frozen to take 'n bake—and I asked all the questions I could. Out of all the pizzas I sampled, ten became my favorites.

When I was 17, the maker of my number-one favorite pizza of all time took me under his wing. That mentorship really gave me a great start in understanding the inside story—the preparation—it took to come up with a really good finished product.

At the age of 24, I finally made my first pizza for my wife and me. My pizza passion grew until we opened a pizza parlor in 1971 in the small town where we lived. I had a full-time job as an insurance adjuster and was able to run the "Pizza Corner" just on Friday, Saturday and Sunday nights.

The restaurant was packed every night we were open, but the building was sold, and the pizza business had to close. That didn't stop me from learning. I continued to get into more and more commercial pizza kitchens to see how different makers produced their pizzas. When tasting something I liked, I either duplicated it or made it even better.

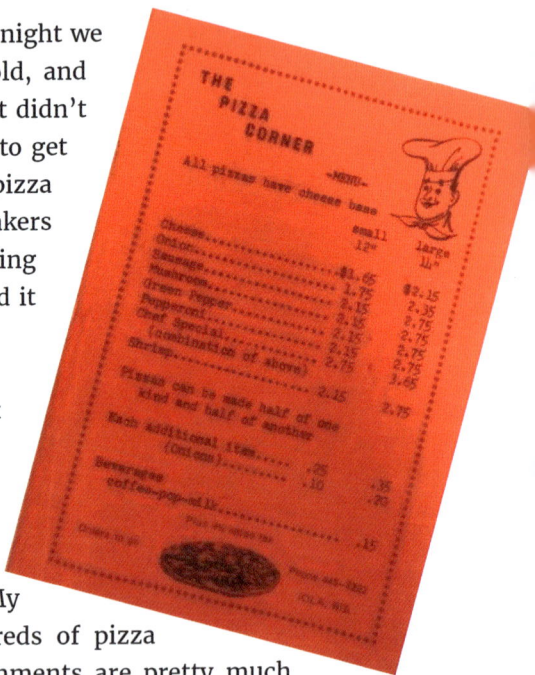

Back at home, I bought commercial pizza equipment for my basement "laboratory" where I experimented to find the best methods, equipment and ingredients for the best pizza. My wife and I have entertained hundreds of pizza parties over the years, and the comments are pretty much the same: "This is the best pizza I have ever had!"

How can you tell when pizza is good? When you can't stop eating it. With this book, I invite you to dive into the art of making one of America's favorite foods while enjoying the education.

Jim "The Pizza Guy"

Table of Contents

THE GREATEST PIZZA ON EARTH STARTS HERE

T his book is not about the history of pizza, nor is it about all the different types of pizza in the world, nor does it have a lot of other information you don't need when it comes to making fabulous pizzas.

My mission—and passion—is simply to teach individuals what they need to know in order to make great conventional pizzas in their own kitchen ovens. This book is written for pizza lovers, for those who are looking for quality, for the families that love pizza but can't afford to eat out as often as they would like, for those who are tired of frozen pizzas, and for those who are concerned about what's in them.

Yes, I know, there are those who can afford to eat fresh pizza out anytime they want, but I have trained several multi-millionaires to make their own pizzas at home. They rarely go out for pizza anymore. It's not about the money. It's just plain better at home.

But if you are thinking about money, home-made pizza is a real value compared to the options. As a rule, the average pizza lover can eat a meal of fresh, delicious, nutritious homemade pizza for $1 per person. That's what it costs if I make a 12-inch plain cheese pizza with 5 ounces of pretty good mozzarella from Costco, and it will feed both my wife and me. That same size pizza at a fresh pizzeria runs $10 to $14. Even if I pay retail for mozzarella from my favorite cheese factory, the 12-inch cheese pizza still comes to only $1.50.

Outside of a fast food burger—which is 1 to 1 ½ ounces of bun and the same weight in meat—where can you eat today for 50 cents or even $1? Making your own great pizza even costs much less than buying the frozen babysitter four-for-$10 pizzas!

A neat thing about making pizza is that anyone can do it, whether you fancy yourself a cook or not. It's a fact, there are a lot of men who are very comfortable in the kitchen, but there are also those whose only place in cooking is at the grill. Pizza will get those grill jockeys into the kitchen. It's just plain fun making pizza. It's not "cooking" as we know it.

If you are used to running the kitchen, be prepared to share the space. This is one food where the entire family will want to get involved. Even kids as young as four can sprinkle cheese. By the time they are a little older, they can do it all. There is no greater reward in the kitchen than watching a youngster's face as their pizza comes out of the oven. They can't wait until it's on the table!

The reason this is not a large book is that there is only so much that needs to be said about the art of making pizzas. You will find the word "simple" used quite a bit in the book, because the ingredients, the equipment and the process are truly simple. Other books tend to complicate the matter.

My goal is to teach you how to make the greatest pizza on earth.

How do I dare make such a bold statement as that? It's easy. We all have different tastes, and as your instructor, I'll get you started on the right track. I will show you the dos and don'ts, the how's and whys, and give you information from my years of experience that most pizza makers don't know.

Once you start following my simple instructions and have a good feel for the art of making pizzas, you can experiment on your own, not only achieving the flavors you like, but also using the exact amounts of sauce, cheese and toppings that will wow your families and friends. Soon you'll be enjoying your personal "greatest pizza on earth."

After all, that's what it's all about; having it the way you like it. As my friend Leonard would say, "It don't get no better than that!"

Chapter 1

WHERE WILL YOUR PIZZA COME FROM?

There are five basic places you can get a pizza these days. There are pros and cons to each. Of course, my favorite is homemade, but let's take a look at all of them.

Fresh from pizzerias

These are the most expensive ($20 to $30 for an extra-large) and typically the best, as they should be. Still, they are a far cry from what they can be. When I was growing up and pizza was new and exciting, I had my own list of the ten top pizzerias in central Wisconsin. Sad to say, the owners have all died or sold out. My opinion is that, with the exception of one, the other nine aren't worth wasting money on. Chains and speed delivery in those steamed pouches, along with coupons and precooked sausage, have all ruined the good name of pizzeria pizza.

In our travels coast to coast, I try pizza wherever we go. I can just look at a pizza and tell if I want a bite or not.

Frozen

Over the years, I have seen a lot of the frozen manufacturers come and go. Still, there are tons of them selling millions of pizzas every day. These pizzas are ready to be baked and can be found in the grocery store freezer section. They come with a wide variety of toppings and crusts. Price and convenience are the two players here. You can pay $6 to $12 for the premium line and four-for-$10 for the economy line.

Take-and-bake

There are several of these businesses around. Someone else assembles the fresh pizza to your order so you can take it home to bake. For those who prefer fresh over frozen, one may consider take-and-bake as convenient, but the price is only slightly below the fresh, sit-down pizzerias. Coupons, promotions and deals put the price all over the board, but without any of that, expect to pay $15 to $20 for an extra-large with a few toppings. It's not a great savings, and you have gas and time invested to go pick it up.

Bar pizza

This is where the bar will typically use fresh toppings but put them on the same type of pre-made crusts used in frozen pizzas, so there's no advantage there, except fresh is always better than frozen. A bar pizza should be priced accordingly, but from what I can see, they are not. Most—but not all—are charging close to fresh pizzeria prices. It is not uncommon to pay $10 to $12 for a 12-inch pizza using precooked sausage, but it is way too much in my book.

Homemade pizza

These pizzas are the ones that you assemble and bake at home. There is a certain amount of preparation and planning involved. They're not as convenient as popping a frozen pizza in the oven. That's the only negative I can think of, if you can call it that. So, let's cover the positives.

- They taste much better than anything you can buy, fresh or frozen.
- They are much healthier for you than all the rest, because you know what's in yours. Read the labels on the frozen, especially the self-rising. It's scary.
- They are much cheaper than any of the other choices, including the four-for-$10 babysitter pizzas.
- There is no tax, tip, travel or soggy delivery.
- They are fun to make, especially if there are kids involved.

This book will introduce you to techniques for making home-baked Chicago, thin crust and Detroit style pizzas.

Chapter 2

SIMPLE INGREDIENTS

The purpose of this book is to get you started on the right track, and because we all have different tastes, you will only find out which product is right for you by trial and error. The beauty of it is, even when testing the various products in search of the ones that are right for you, your pizzas will all be edible, and most likely still better than anything you get when eating out.

Dough

Dough is the basis for a really good pizza and deserves more space than this short introduction. You'll find everything you need in Chapter 4, including my simple dough formula, mixing methods, challenges with added ingredients, and options for whole wheat and gluten-free crusts.

Sauce

There's a large variety of tomato products available. Tomato products used for pizza are puree, crushed tomato and 6-in-1 All Purpose Ground. Use a combination of puree and one of the other two, or add salsa if making a taco pizza.

The tomato products are available in 28-ounce cans and range in price from $1.60 to$2.60 a can. When shopping at grocery stores, a few brands I really like are Contadina crushed, Escalon 6-in-1 All Purpose Ground and Hunts tomato puree.

For those who want the absolute best, look for Stanislaus Full-Red Tomato Puree. It is available in #10 cans online but will be hard to find in that size anywhere else (I buy it wholesale through a pizza parlor). Webrestaurantstore.com sells the puree for under $6, which is very affordable, but added shipping comes into play. Amazon.com has it for under $18 and can be a better deal for Prime members. Stanislaus has many other products, but they can be pretty pricey. The puree is the one I can recommend. It is easy to portion the contents into 1- or 2-pound plastic containers and freeze them. Just pull out what you want the day before it is needed, and let it thaw in the refrigerator. You'll find more about sauces in chapter 5.

Cheese

Quality mozzarella is fine, but a good cheese combination is mozzarella with 10% to 20% provolone blended for added flavor. You won't taste the cheese as much as you will notice its performance. The right cheese should have excellent body and a wonderful stretch...what pizza makers call "string." Spots of browning on the baked pizza are fine, but I prefer white and creamy. Hard cheeses are another option. Parmesan, Romano or Asiago are a few of the main ones that will give your pizzas an even bigger flavor boost.

Provolone makes a nice flavor combination with Mozzarella and performs well on a pizza.

I like to blend a little mild cheddar when doing my taco pizza. Better yet, for those who want the best and aren't concerned with price (shipping costs come in to play), Burnett Dairy's 80-10-10 blend is perfect and works well on any pizza. See more about cheese in Chapter 6.

Meats

Meat toppings can be anything you imagine. Some of the standards are Italian sausage (season your own using my formulas or buy pre-seasoned), pepperoni (pork or turkey made by Hormel are good), ham, bacon, Canadian bacon, salami, and chicken leftovers from a meal or grilling. Find more ideas in Chapter 7.

Spices/Herbs

The standard spices are salt, garlic salt, garlic cloves, ground black pepper, leaf oregano, and crushed red pepper for extra heat. Spices don't last forever, so I don't recommend buying large quantities. They lose power the older they get.

You can make your own garlic salt by mixing one part granulated garlic with ten parts table salt. I like refrigerating garlic salt for freshness and anti-caking.

My favorite oregano is Greek oregano because of its outstanding flavor. I'm very happy with Zane-Hellas as a supplier.

Other toppings

Canned or fresh mushrooms, onion, green pepper, and black and green olives are all the old traditional choices, but don't stop there. Other less traditional toppings you might want to try are sweet peppers, hot peppers, broccoli, anchovies or whatever comes to mind. If you like it, that's all that counts.

When using canned mushrooms, rinse them in a strainer and press out any excess liquid. For a crispy crust, we want our toppings as dry as possible. Wet toppings can make a soggy crust.

As a rule of thumb, go light on the toppings. If you have more than 5, you have a casserole, not a pizza. There are topping recipes and tips in Chapter 8.

Chapter 3

PANS, ACCESSORIES AND OTHER EQUIPMENT

There are a few items you will want to find in your kitchen or purchase before making great pizzas at home. A few items are optional, and you'll learn why in the following chapters, but using the best equipment is important. For instance, you probably won't be able to make the best pizzas with the typical pans found in most kitchens today.

Pans

Most non-commercial pizza makers wouldn't have a clue what to buy when it comes to pans and other tools for making great pizza, and neither did I without a lot of trial and error. I spent over $3,000 testing all kinds of baking pans from different manufacturers. I found that light-weight, low-quality pans won't give you anywhere near the consistently golden brown crispy crust you want. I found the best pans at LloydPans in Spokane, WA.

They are "easy release" which means the surface material is non-toxic, unlike the coatings on many commodity non-stick pans which break down at the high temperatures needed for good pizza crusts. According to LloydPans, their dark surface and thicker construction transfers heat more evenly and makes for a crispier crust. I agree.

There are four styles of pans used in this book: cutter pans for thin-crust pizza, 2-inch (round) deep dish for Chicago style, square pans for Detroit style, and round 1 ½ -inch deep pans for garlic strips. The garlic strip pan is the same as a Chicago style pan but not as deep.

Once you buy commercial, quality pans and take proper care of them, they should last you a lifetime. Quality is not cheap, so order what you can, even if one at a time. Another thing to consider is the cost of shipping.

If you have small children at home, I recommend one or two of the 10-inch thin crust pans so each child can make his own. You can use the same one over of course, but it has to cool down first.

For beginner adults and older children who are making their own, please start with the 10-inch or medium 13-inch pan before tackling the extra-large 15-inch. It takes practice handling dough, and it's much easier learning with the smaller pizzas.

LloydPans makes a wide variety of pans, so I have tried to make it as easy as I can with the recommendations below. You can see their selection and order online at https://lloydpans.com, or call (800) 748-6251 and give them your item numbers.

As a special deal, LloydPans is offering a 10% discount if you order online and use my Promotion Code 10HPP. For convenience, go to my LloydPans web page at https://lloydpans.com/home-pizza-parlor.html, where you will also see many more photos of the pizza process.

THIN CRUST "CUTTER" PANS
They are called cutter pans because the edges are designed so excess dough can be trimmed, or cut, after the pizza is made. It's a great built-in feature.

These are outside measurements. The actual pizza is one inch less. Prices shown are as of December 2019 (prices subject to change).

10" H63N-10 X .75-PSTK	$15.18
13" H63N-13 X .75-PSTK	21.50
15" H63N-15 X .75-PSTK	25.29
16" H63N-16 X .75-PSTK	35.40

1.5" DEEP DISH (NESTING)
I use these for garlic strips.

10" H76R-10 X 1.5-PSTK $9.28
13" H76R-13 X 1.5-PSTK 12.28

2" DEEP DISH (NESTING)
These are for Chicago style pizzas.

10" H76R-10 X 2-PSTK $9.28
13" H76R-13 X 2-PSTK 12.28

DETROIT SQUARE PAN
8 X 10" RCT-14927-PSTK $23.74
10 X 14" RCT-14926-PSTK 30.29

Pan grippers for thin crust

This tool makes it much easier to get a hot pizza pan out of the oven without getting your oven mitt or pot holder in the topping. LloydPans has them for just under $15, which is a little pricey. A less expensive source is Northern Pizza Equipment (https://www.northenpizzaequipment.com).

You can also buy most other accessories from Northern, like the grippers for the cutter pan and deep dish pans, and plastic covers for square pans, which are about $3.50 for an 8 X 10" and $5.50 for 10 X 14".

Other equipment

Electronic scale

Inexpensive ones are available that measure ounces and grams. For weighing flour and dough, ounces down to the tenth place works fine. If you are making Italian sausage at home, look for a more accurate scale that measure in grams to the hundredth place.

An electronic scale is more accurate for measuring small amounts, like spices for sausage.

Serving trays or cardboard pizza circles

If you serve your pizza on an aluminum tray, be sure it is warmed or put a parchment layer between the pizza and the tray so the bottom of the crust doesn't sweat and get soggy. Another option is ready-made cardboard circles.

Parchment paper

This serves as a sweat barrier when using aluminum serving trays.

Rolling pins

Either a standard wood or aluminum rolling pin will work for rolling out the dough balls. If using the cutter pans for your thin crust pizza you will also want a small rolling pin to trim the excess dough from the cutter pan.

A special small roller for trimming excess dough works well for cutter pans.

Ladle or wide spoon holding 2 or 3 ounces

This is for applying measured amounts of sauce.

Food processor or stand mixer

Dough can be mixed by hand too. If you don't own either mixer, I recommend the processor. It's a lot less money and much faster. See more in Chapter 4.

Mix dough by hand or with a food processor (left) or stand mixer (right)

Food storage bags, 1-gallon size

I prefer simple twist-tie bags over ones that zip shut. For one thing, they are less expensive. It is also easier to squeeze all the air out before tying them shut.

Bench brush

This is a soft bristle brush used for sweeping away flour from the counter top and rolled dough circles.

Pizza cutter

A 4-inch wheel works best. Metal is preferred, but either metal or plastic is fine.

Baking stone or steel

If you are not baking in a pan, you need a baking surface with a high thermal mass that bakes evenly. Baking steels that slide into your oven are available online. Pizza stones are round or rectangular and are generally made of ceramic or stone to sit directly on the oven shelf. My experience with a $40 stone was that it didn't give me the browning I wanted, and it lost so much heat after the first bake that it needed 20 more minutes of reheating at 500 degrees for the next round. I wasn't impressed, but I recently discovered the Weber Grilling Stone (#8829), which works great on a grill and probably would in an oven too. If you buy a stone or steel, be sure it is big enough for your pizza and small enough for your oven.

Peels

This is a flat paddle-shaped tool for working with stone or steel-baked pizzas. A wood peel is used when assembling the pizza and metal peel for removing it from the oven.

Garlic peeler and press

While these tools are by no means critical to making good pizza, they are handy tools that can make the job go more quickly. To use the peeler, slide a few garlic bulbs into the tube and set it flat on a counter beneath the palm of your hand. Put a little pressure on the tube as you roll it back and forth several times against the counter top. The papery garlic skins peel right off. Clean cloves can be popped into the press to squeeze juice onto your favorite topping.

A rubber garlic peeler (left) and garlic press (right) are handy tools for the home pizza maker.

Dough Docker

This tool is a short-handled roller with metal or plastic spines used when parbaking crusts. It is rolled over the surface of the raw rolled dough before it is baked to prevent bubbling.

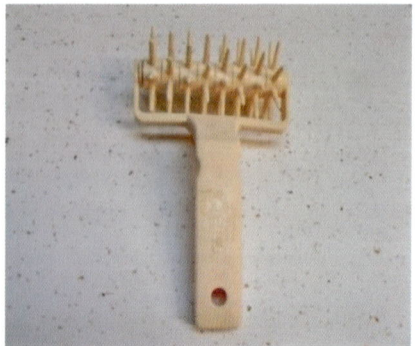

Chapter 4

THE DOUGH / CRUST

The majority of pizza lovers will say the crust is the most important part of the pizza, and I agree! The biggest problem folks seem to have in making their pizza is in producing a good, quality crust. But take heart; you will find that will no longer be a problem.

I'm spending a lot of time in this very important area, but don't think it's because it's difficult to make really good dough. We just have several areas to cover. Once you've gone through the process a couple of times, you will see it's really quite easy.

Over the years, I did everything I could think of to come up with the ultimate crust. It had to be tasty and tender, yet crispy on the outside. Through hundreds of experiments of trial and error, using various ingredients and quantities, I feel that I achieved what I set out to do, and that's what I'm sharing with you in this book.

Although there are pizzerias that work with a "hot" or fresh dough, I don't. Doughs that don't require aging never appealed to me. Aging creates body, texture and flavor. The ultimate crust requires a little planning ahead, but once you see through that, you can't help but love the process. Once you see how this simple process works, you will quickly get over any pre-planning jitters.

Most dough formulas are way too complicated and take too much time to make, plus they don't turn out good. And, if you are looking for several different dough formulas, you won't find them here. One very simple and really good dough formula will give you a nice, brown, tasty, crispy crust for the various styles of pizza in my book. Still, each will taste different because of the pans that are used.

I will also teach you how to handle your pizza dough so that you always have dough balls ready to roll out when the need arises. Freezing your excess dough is totally unnecessary when following my process, and frozen dough will not perform the same as fresh.

For those who don't want to mess with the most important part of the pizza and would rather buy commercial pre-made crusts, think twice. You will not only pay almost as much for just the crust than it takes to make the entire pizza from scratch, but you will also miss out on a far superior end result. Pre-made crust is also full of stuff like dough conditioners and preservatives that improve its shelf life but not the flavor.

There is no comparison in any shape or form between a purchased crust and my scratch dough formula.

Three ways to make dough

We can make dough using a **food processor**, which is the fastest way, and it's what I recommend. A serviceable food processor will cost $50 to $60. There are more expensive machines if you so choose, but they shouldn't be necessary. A 12-cup processor is just the right size for my dough formula. Although a 10-cup will work, it's just barely large enough, and a 14-cup is overkill. I use a Hamilton Beach.

Another mechanical option is a **stand mixer**, such as a KitchenAid. They run around $200. Besides costing more, they take much longer to mix than does a food processor.

Then there is the **hand-kneading** method, such as the old timers used when making bread three times a week for their large families. If you are going to mix by hand and haven't done any yeast doughs before, check a cookbook, research online, or ask a bread-making friend to show you how to mix and knead bread ingredients by hand.

My "simple" dough formula
17 oz. bread flour (approx. 3 ½ cups)
½ tsp. instant (rapid rise) yeast
10 oz. cool (80 degrees) tap water (1 ¼ cups)

Flour, water and yeast make up my simple dough formula, but let's look at the ingredients individually.

Flour
Bread flour is recommended. Its higher protein content creates a stronger dough and crispier crust, but all-purpose flour will also work. The result will be a softer crust. You can try different brands and stick with what you like, but they are all very similar. You might want to just shop by price.

Yeast
Most dough formulas suggest using active dry yeast, but it requires rehydrating, which takes time and is totally unnecessary. I recommend instant (rapid rise) yeast, which can be mixed directly in with the flour and water. In the end, you will never taste the difference, but you will save yourself a bunch of unnecessary monkeying around.

Instant yeast is often found in 4-ounce jars. Although you should be able to make approximately 64 batches of dough from one jar, it's pricey in that quantity. A jar ranges from $8 to $10. Instant yeast is also found in three-pack sachets, each packet holding about 4 ½ teaspoons of yeast. That's enough for 4 batches of dough and will cost $1.60 to $1.75. It's an equivalent price to the jar. You can also buy it in vacuum sealed 1-pound packages in some stores for less than $5. My favorite—SAF-Instant—is available for sale online. Pour the contents into a storage container, keep it tightly sealed in the freezer, and pull out smaller quantities as you need. If you have active dry yeast on hand, by all means use it up, but then switch to instant.

Although all we used in the bakery was fresh (cake) yeast, I don't find any advantage in using the fresh yeast in pizza dough. Any yeast will work just fine, but the instant requires the least amount of work. If you choose to use cake yeast, a scant ¼ ounce is plenty. Just dissolve it in the water, then whisk it around and mix with the flour.

Water

Rumor has it that New York pizza crusts are great because of their water. Personally, I was not impressed with New York pizza and am not sure what all the hype is about the crust? If the "great water" theory is true, then why did my number 1 pizzeria of all time have the greatest crust of all and the worst city water I have ever tasted? Their water was heavily loaded with chlorine, and my mentor did not filter it. You can try softened or unsoftened, filtered or unfiltered, and see what you like best. In other words, taste is not the biggest concern when it comes to water. The real concerns are quantity and temperature.

This is one area where a scale comes in very handy. I have discovered that not all measuring cups are created equal. One cup of water weighs 8 ounces, and we use 10 ounces to a single batch of dough. That amount should measure on the 1 ¼ measuring line, but not all cups are "lined" properly. So, weigh your water the first time and see where 10 ounces measure on your cup. It may be a little above or below the 1 ¼ cup line. If you don't have a scale, you will have to find out by trial and error. Keep notes. The proper amount is critical!

The water temperature also makes a difference. It should be just cool (80 degrees). Overly hot water could kill the yeast. If warm, the dough will just rise quicker; too cold, and it will really slow down the rising process.

High altitude pizza

I've never baked at high altitudes, so if you're one of those who does, you may have to adjust the formula and baking times slightly. Experiment and keep notes.

The lowdown on salt, sugar and oil

I don't care for "thick and chewy," but if that's the type of crust you prefer, the basic recipe will need adjustments. Add a teaspoon of salt, two teaspoons of sugar and double the yeast. Salt tenderizes the dough and also retards fermentation big time. I consider both to be bad qualities and don't want either in my pizza dough.

If salt is left out of the dough formula, the dough needs to be worked cold, right out of the refrigerator. When it warms up, the dough will become sticky and hard to handle. Of course, if you are adding salt to get a softer crust, the temperature won't matter. Salt tenderizes dough, makes it less sticky and ends with a stronger dough and chewy crust.

In the end, the finished product will tell you what to add and what to leave out. After baking your pizza, just smell the crust, and you will smell the purity of an unadulterated tasty crust. Do the same sniff test when you eat out, and it won't be long before you stop eating out and stay at home making better pizzas and enjoying them more.

Sugar does nothing for flavoring the dough, unless you are making a sweet dough like cinnamon rolls and use a lot of it. The two things sugar does do is provide food for the yeast so the dough will rise and aid in browning the crust. When we don't use any salt in the formula, it is totally unnecessary to add sugar to aid in the rising process, plus you will find your crust will brown nicely without it.

You may add a tablespoon of your choice of oil also, to soften the dough. In days of old, you never heard much about olive oil, at least not that I was aware of, and now that's all you hear. Just keep in mind that some oils, like olive and sesame seed, will add their own flavors to the finished product. If that's what you want, fine. Most pizza parlors used a vegetable oil or maybe a solid shortening to soften the dough if desired, but please, start with my simple formula. It may be all the farther you'll want to go.

If you do play with adding oil, some experts say don't add it to the water, but wait until the dough starts to combine. It's true that oil and water don't mix.

Wheat dough
In order to be whole wheat, you must use 100% whole wheat flour, which doesn't work too well. It lacks gluten and forms a weak, dry crust. For a nice dough, I recommend using just 1/3 to 1/2 whole wheat flour and the remainder white bread flour. That combination actually handles and rolls out better than all white flour. Instructions for mixing wheat flour are the same as all white.

Mixing dough using a stand mixer
When using a stand mixer, it takes about 10 minutes of actual mixing from the time the ingredients begin to combine.
Measure the ingredients out before you start. Pour the water in the mixer bowl, dump the flour and instant yeast in, twist the dough hook in place, twist and lock the bowl on the mixer, lower and lock the motor head and mix the ingredients on the second speed until combined.

Continue mixing on second speed for ten minutes. If the dough climbs the hook or isn't grabbing on the hook, stop the mixer, raise the head and push the ball of dough down. Relock the head into place and continue kneading until the dough has gone the full 10 minutes. You can make just short of a double batch using the stand mixer. For the larger batch, use 2 cups (16 ounces) water, 27 ounces flour and 1 teaspoon yeast. This will give you 43 ounces of dough when done.

Remove the finished dough from the mixer. At this point, the dough should not stick to the fingers. If it does, return the ball to the mixer with a tablespoon of flour and knead until the flour is completely incorporated. Repeat if necessary. Form a ball and seal it in a large plastic food storage bag for refrigeration.

Mixing the dough using a food processor

Most folks don't know they can use a food processor for mixing yeast doughs, but nothing could be faster or easier than mixing your pizza dough with one of these high speed machines.

Measure out your flour, water and yeast. Dump the flour and yeast into the bowl, then pour water over the top. Replace the cover, pulse a few times, and then hit the high speed button. If your measurements are right on, the dough should form quite quickly. When it starts to combine, continue processing at high speed for approximately 15 seconds.

Mixing time doesn't really matter until the ingredients start to pull together into a ball. That's when you start timing. You will be able to see when the dough combines, plus you will hear the food processor working harder.

If the dough is not combining within half a minute, remove the cover and push the dough down closer to the blade. Note the consistency. If it is too sticky, add one tablespoon of flour. If too dry, add one tablespoon of water. Return the cover, and start processing again. If it still isn't right, repeat the process. Dough that is too dry or too wet won't combine well. Only with practice will you know how good dough should feel.

If the dough is too stiff (too dry), it can burn out the food processor motor. You will hear it groan while mixing. Stiff dough is also much harder to roll out. A scale for ingredients is really important!

After the dough has mixed for 15 seconds, remove the ball and blade from the processor bowl. Remember that the blade is razor sharp. If there is any dough sticking to it, touch the pieces with the finished ball of dough, and they will pull away. "Round up" the dough ball as explained below and seal in a large plastic food storage bag for refrigeration.

Remember to clean the processor immediately while the dough is soft. Rinse out the inside of the blade, place the blade back in the bowl, then fill the bowl with soap and hot water to soften. I rinse the lid off with hot water, then after 5 minutes or so, using a toothbrush, I clean the blade off and wash the bowl out with a dish pad. I don't want to come near the blade with my fingers! It can take as long to clean the machine as it does to make the dough, but it's really only a few minutes.

Rounding up the dough ball
Once the ingredients have been mixed into a rough ball, pull the edges of the dough under several times from the outside in, using both hands to "round it up" into a smooth, tight ball.

Part of the dough will be noticeably warmer than the rest. Keep pulling the dough under until blended with the cooler portion. Once tucked into a smooth ball, pinch the bottom seam tightly together. (If the dough is too wet and sticky, it will be hard to handle when it is rounded into balls and when it comes time to roll it out.)

Seal each dough ball in a large food storage bag and place it seam-side down on a dish towel or other cloth surface in the refrigerator. This will reduce chilling on the bottom of the dough. Use a plate or other flat surface under the dough ball if the refrigerator has wire shelves.

Depending on your situation, you may want to make two or even three batches of dough. Remember, one batch makes three medium pizzas or two extra-large, so it's easy to plan. This pizza dough keeps 10 days or more in the refrigerator when rounded up every two or three days.

Dough balls rest on a towel in the refrigerator to protect their bottoms from chilling. Different colored twist ties identify the weight of each ball, which corresponds to the size pizza each will produce.

Allowing time for the dough balls to rise

Give the dough a full day to rise slowly in the refrigerator to double its original size, then remove and divide into three 9-ounce dough balls or two 13-ounce dough balls. Either write on zipper closure bags or use different color twist-ties to differentiate between the dough balls; like white for small, red for medium and green for extra-large.

Return the dough to the refrigerator for another 24 hours of proofing. An ice cold refrigerator might chill the yeast so much that the dough doesn't rise. If that should be the case, try slightly warmer water and increase the yeast to one teaspoon the next time.

The bottom line to the proofing stage is that it makes it easier to roll out the dough balls. They must be full of air bubbles, or you will be fighting a dead horse. If the dough is hard to roll, allow it to proof longer the next time. There are a lot of good things going on during this aging process which are so important for great taste and a great crust. Don't be disheartened. You will find handling dough in this manner is not as time consuming as it may sound. It takes only a minute or two to round them up as they age, and the reward far exceeds any work involved.

Pizzerias would have a problem rolling out their dough if they didn't go through a similar proofing process. The only difference in a commercial operation is that most of their dough balls get consumed right away, and what's left over gets re-rolled just one more time.

There are some operations like Dominos that receive their dough balls proofed in boxes from their commissary and are ready to work. They don't use an electronic roller but rather push the dough out with their fingers. Others spin the dough in the air. It all has the same end result and is called sheeting the dough.

At home, we have the time it takes to make our pizzas like Pizza Hut did in their humble beginning, by rolling them out from fresh dough made on site.

Pizza dough is very different from other yeast doughs when it comes to shelf life. It will keep in the refrigerator for ten days or even more if you handle the dough balls properly. Here's what most home pizza makers—and some pros—don't know. Let's say you made your dough Monday night and let it rise for a day, then Tuesday night divided it into three smaller dough balls for three medium pizzas. If they rise for another day as instructed, there are three dough balls ready to roll out Wednesday.

Let's say you make just one pizza on Wednesday night and have two dough balls left. If you make a second pizza on Thursday night, you will find it rolls out even easier, because the gluten chains have relaxed a little longer. You have one dough ball left. If you plan on using it on Friday, it will still be okay. Otherwise, take it out on Thursday night and round it up again. Place it back in the same storage bag and use it Friday, Saturday or even Sunday night.

If you do not use the last dough ball up by Sunday night, just round it up again as before. This process can continue until the dough turns grey and doesn't rise anymore. It's amazing how long your dough will last when handling it in this manner. I will typically have 1 to 3 dough balls ready to roll out at all times. If you don't have any dough ready on-demand, there can't be any pizza for supper!

I re-use the plastic bags. I gently remove the dough balls from the bags, allowing them to turn inside out. They are dry a day later, and I can shake the dough flakes out and use the bag again.

Rush batch of dough

There are always those days when something comes up and you need to speed the process. The best dough will always be the one that has plenty of time to rise and proof, but there are ways to shorten the preparation time that still result in a darned good pizza.

One option cuts the prep time to about 36 hours. Starting early in the morning, use slightly warmer water (85 degrees), double the yeast, then bag the dough and put it. in the refrigerator. Don't let the dough get too warm by using very warm water unless salt is added to control yeast activity. The dough should rise and be ready to divide into smaller portions by that evening. Put the divided dough balls back into the refrigerator to proof and be ready to make pizzas the next night.

Gluten free

There are pizza lovers who can't eat wheat—or choose not to for one reason or another—and need gluten-free flour. There are a few alternatives. Bob's Red Mill is one of several brands that offers gluten free (GF) pizza mix that just needs water. It costs considerably more than conventional bread flour, but it's an option.

Another is cauliflower crust, which can either be bought or made from scratch. Anytime you make your own anything, you can count on saving money, plus they should be better tasting. The downside is that it's a lot of work. The internet is a good source for both cauliflower dough recipes and commercially available cauliflower rice.

For another easy and inexpensive idea, leave the crust to the rest of the family, and eat the toppings.

Par-baked crusts

This method takes a few extra ingredients and a few extra tools, and it makes a totally different product, but it's a pretty good pizza in the end. You'll need a wood pizza peel, a metal pizza peel, a bench brush, and either a baking stone or a steel baking surface.

When I make these I don't even proof my dough balls, but I have a commercial dough roller which makes that possible. If rolling by hand, you will have to have proofed dough balls as described earlier in this chapter.

There won't be any trimming with this method, so after the first rise, reduce the weight of the dough balls by 3 ounces and start with 6 ounces for a medium size pizza.

Preheat the oven and stone or steel baking surface to 500 degrees.

A parbaked crust may develop bubbles during its initial bake. Remove it from the oven with a steel peel and flatten the crust with something like two cardboard pizza circles. It can also be pierced with a dough docker before baking.

After rolling out the dough, slide it onto the stone using a wood peel, and allow it to bake a minute or two to bubble up. Let the dough come up ½ to 1 inch, and if you get a big bubble, it's ok. The bubbles won't be "even" nor do they have to be. Remove the crust with a steel peel.

Place crust on a flat surface and flatten with whatever you have that will do the trick. I use two pizza circles. Cool, and with a bench brush, brush the excess flour off both sides. Several of these can be made ahead and stored in tightly sealed plastic bags in the refrigerator or freezer until needed. No need to defrost; just add toppings and bake as usual right on the oven rack, stone or steel surface.

One challenge with this method is that par-baked pizza crusts sometimes bake up with big bubbles that can cause the toppings to slide around. Just pop them as they appear. Another option is to roll over the crusts with a dough docker before baking them.

Rolling out the Dough

There isn't a whole lot to know about rolling out a dough ball, but you do need to know a few important details that I'll share with you.

Once your dough has risen a couple of times and your dough balls are fully proofed, you are ready to roll out a dough ball for any of the styles of pizza you're making. The deep dish, garlic strips, pan style and square pan are easier to roll out since we don't roll them out as thin.

Start out by wearing short sleeve shirts anytime you're in the kitchen, and it doesn't hurt to have a cap on too. Even on the high class TV shows, I see chefs with long sleeves, sometimes rolled up, but why not start out the right way?

After cleaning your counter top with a disinfectant cleaner and thoroughly washing your hands, heavily dust some flour on the area where you will roll out the dough. Place the dough ball on the floured area and cover the top of the dough ball with more flour. Don't worry about how much you are using; the dough will absorb only as much as it can take, and you don't want it to stick to hands or equipment. With your hand, press down on the dough, squeezing all the air out.

When pressing down on the dough ball, the air should whoosh out leaving the dough ball quite flat. If it doesn't flatten out, the dough hasn't relaxed enough and will be more difficult to work with. If your dough balls haven't risen as well as they should, maybe you didn't give them quite enough time or your refrigerator is too cold. Take them out early, and let them warm up for 2 to 3 hours, but then put them back in the 'fridge to cool down again before rolling. Dough must always be cold when working it, unless you use salt. Warm unsalted dough is sticky. After you've practiced with the dough a few times, you will know how it should look and feel before rolling.

Assuming your dough ball is deflated and ready to go, pick the dough up and spread more flour on the counter. Place the dough back on the floured surface, and dust the top with flour again. With your rolling pin, roll the dough out to the size you want. As soon as it fights you and won't roll out any further, stop rolling. You won't win that one!

Lift the dough again, repeat spreading the flour around on the counter and on top of the dough, and let it rest 5 to 10 minutes. After it relaxes, the dough will roll out the rest of the way quite easily. You always want your oven, pans, sauces and other ingredients ready when you start rolling out the dough balls, but while it's resting, you might find something else that needs to be done.

When the ball has been rolled out to the desired size, take your bench brush and brush the excess flour off both sides of the dough. It is now ready for whichever pan style you're baking. If you're baking on a stone (no pan), then I suggest just brushing off the top of the dough and gently shaking off the bottom. A little flour on the bottom side will help it slide off the wood peel better.

Chapter 5

THE SAUCES

S auce is where the flavor is folks, and it's very simple to make.

Years ago we had a frozen pizza manufacturer who advertised on TV, "The secret's in the sauce!" I can't disagree with that statement. After you make a great crust, sauce comes in a close second. Back then, I traveled 60 miles each way to buy one of those advertised pizzas and met one of the owners. I didn't care for their pizza, and I must not have been the only one, since they went out of business a few years later.

Most individuals, along with many professionals, over-season their sauce, as was the case with the frozen pizza I bought. First of all, pizza makers, in general, don't cook pizza sauce. Unlike a great pasta sauce, pizza sauce does not require any simmering. There is no advantage to doing that. This is about as simple as sauce can get.

Thirty years ago, a chemist in a huge spice lab taught me a very valuable lesson: "Simply season." He told me that we shouldn't be able to identify any one spice in what we are eating, unless it's the featured item, like garlic in garlic sticks. When you learn this valuable lesson, you will be on your way to making great pizza sauces.

No-seasoning is better than over-seasoning.

Tomato sauce
There are dozens of canned tomato products to experiment with, and until you find what you and your family like best, here is a good starting point. You can't go wrong using tomato puree for your base, but you might want to thin it down with water or crushed tomato or a 6-1 product. Thinning with tomato will give you a richer flavor. If cost is a factor, stay with water. If you use crushed tomato or 6-1 product as your sauce, it is ready to go and doesn't need further thinning. Some

people like to add a teaspoon of sugar to crushed tomatoes. There is more about tomato products in Chapter 2 "The Simple Ingredients."

My simple sauce seasoning formula
28 oz. tomato puree
1 ½ tsp. salt
¼ tsp. garlic salt
1/8 tsp. ground black pepper
2 tsp. leaf oregano or basil, but not both

Empty the puree into a larger container, rinse the can and fill it 1/3 full of water (or with one of the suggested tomato products). Mix that into the puree. If it's too thick, add a little more liquid. The right consistency will slowly run off the ladle or spoon. Once you've done it a few times, you'll know how much liquid works for you.

Stir in the seasonings and you have pizza sauce! Season the sauce at least two hours beforehand for the seasonings to work. Several hours in advance is even better.

Not everyone likes oregano. If that's the case, leave it out of the sauce mix. If some in your family do enjoy the flavor but others don't, just sprinkle it on top of the cheese on part of the pizza.

When I use Contadina crushed tomatoes, I add a teaspoon of sugar, ¼ teaspoon of garlic salt and sometimes a teaspoon of table salt to a can of tomato. I especially like it on the deep dish styles with a sprinkle of oregano over the top of the sauce before baking.

As you experiment with the variety of tomato products available, take notes and keep comments on what you like or don't like. Even if you're not crazy about the one you used this time, you will still be able to eat and enjoy a pizza that tastes better than buying a commercial one.

Hard cheeses are heavy in salt, so if you like the flavor of Parmesan, Asiago or Romano on top, you might want less salt in the sauce. It can always be sprinkled on the sauce or cheese before baking or by the slice afterwards.

The bottom line to seasoning the sauce, pizza lovers, is if you don't go crazy with the spices, you will be way ahead of the rest of the crowd! Start out easy. Whether it is the amount or the kind of spice, please make only one change at a time so you can keep track of what you've done. Take notes.

Taco sauce

To a can of puree—quantity depends on how much sauce you are making—add about a half can of prepared salsa or taco sauce. I like Pace Picante medium. There is also mild or hot, which is extremely hot. The only seasoning you need to add to this is salt to taste.

Barbeque sauce

Most people buy Sweet Baby Rays or other commercial sauces, which are really sweet. What I do is add ¼ teaspoon of fresh cayenne pepper to a 28-ounce bottle of the sauce. This is sometimes hard to spread with a ladle or even a broad spoon, but clean fingers work great.

White sauce

This is basically a ranch dressing, but we're talking pizza topping here. Make your own or buy it, but I like squeezing in 2 to 3 large cloves of fresh garlic per pizza. This is another sauce that can be hard to spread with a ladle or spoon. Again, clean fingers do a fine job.

Chicken, broccoli and onion are a nice topping combo with white sauce.

Chapter 6

THE CHEESE

There's only so much to say about pizza cheese, but I will share with you the important things you should know.

Mozzarella

When it comes to pizza, mozzarella is the key player here, and it's more about the performance of the cheese than the flavor.

There are basically two types of mozzarella; part-skim (2% butterfat) and whole milk, (3% butterfat). In my opinion, whole milk is the best melting, chewing, creamy, performance cheese there is for pizza. The only way for you to know which you like best is to try both.

The average person buys pre-shredded mozzarella, which is the easy way to go, but when it comes to quality, you can't beat buying mozzarella in block form and slicing or shredding it yourself. Pre-shredded packaged cheese includes ingredients like potato starch or cellulose (powdered wood pulp) to keep the shreds from sticking together. That is something to consider.

Mozzarella can be purchased in block form or pre-shredded. If you are not going to shred your own cheese at home, get the best quality pre-shredded product you can find.

My recipes call for either freshly shredded cheese or slices. What is the difference, and why do some pizza operators use sliced rather than shredded?

- Sliced cheese produces a better product, in my book, and will give you more "string" when you lift a hot slice of pizza or take a bite.

- The slices are a consistent thickness, so there is no need to weigh the cheese before applying them to your pizza. I like my slices to weigh 5/8 ounces, which will give me the end result I like. I've got a deli-style electric cheese slicer so I know what adjustment I need to get the right thickness. Most pizza operators will slice theirs at ¾ ounces or more, giving them a cheesier pizza. Plus, thicker slices are easier to handle.

- You want your pizzas to be uniform. If using shreds, you must weigh them. All chains do; many independents don't.

- Raw sausage will come off your fingers and stick to slices much better than to shreds. It's awkward and messy when meat sticks to your fingers and pulls up a wad of shredded cheese instead of dropping neatly onto the pizza. (Here's a tip: Before picking up raw sausage, dip your fingers in the sauce. The meat won't stick to your fingers. This works no matter in what order you choose to assemble the pizza.)

While slices are better for these reasons, some recipes use shredded. For the best results with shredded cheese, shred your own at home or buy a high quality cheese as mentioned below.

Mozzarella is a semi-soft cheese, and it gets softer with age, which means that when it's too old (5 weeks is the absolute limit), the cheese will be too soft and sticky to slice or shred. It also tends to be runny on the pizza, and there isn't any body left when biting into it. The age of block mozzarella is critical, and when buying in the store, you don't have much choice, nor is it labeled. If you must buy cheese in a grocery store, squeeze the block. If it's soft (which most likely it will be), it's older than you want.

Burnett Dairy, a farmer-owned cooperative in northern Wisconsin, offers one of the finest mozzarellas I know of. Their website is https://www.burnettdairy.com. The very best are the 6-pound blocks. If you order from them, call 3 weeks in advance to get it young. I find that 2 to 4 weeks old is the perfect age. Five weeks old would be the maximum you'd want to use.

Six-pound blocks can be cut into roughly 1-pound pieces. Wrap and refrigerate what you will be using right away. Tightly wrap the others with plastic and then aluminum foil before freezing. (Freezing stops the aging process.) Vacuum sealing before freezing works well too. Defrost pieces in the refrigerator a day before you need them.

Burnett has an excellent 80-10-10 blend if you want pre-shredded. It is 80% part-skim mozzarella, 10% provolone and 10% cheddar. I can live without the cheddar, but it performs well. I believe you can buy plain shredded 2% or 3% mozzarella from Burnett as well. Burnett's Provolone is an award winning cheese, and mixing 10% to 20% with their mozzarella is a nice blend.

I recently ran into another great source here in Wisconsin, Vern's Cheese (www.vernscheese.com/retail-store/). They have a huge variety of cheeses and are happy to ship. Grande Cheese is a major player in Italian cheeses, and Vern's carries Grande's three blend cheese in shredded 5-pound packages. It is 2% mozzarella, plus a mixture of provolone and white cheddar.

No doubt there are other cheese factories to buy from, but I can vouch for Burnett and Vern's products. I've had plenty of poor performing mozzarella from other cheese factories, but all you can do is try them and find out. Grocery store cheeses never meet my expectations, with the exception of Costco's shredded mozzarella. It is less expensive and performs well, but I buy it only when I run out of my favorites from Burnett Dairy and Vern's.

Hard cheeses
I do not buy grated hard cheese in a green can. Fifty years ago it had flavor and aroma. Now it has additives and not much flavor. I generally buy solid chunks of the aged, hard cheese and freshly grate it at home, but I have also found that Grande and Vern's have very good grated cheeses.

Hard cheeses have more salt than mozzarella. As mentioned in chapter 5, you might want to consider reducing the salt in your sauce formula when using these cheeses.

One final note on cheese
St. Louis is known for its own processed cheese concoction called Provel. I'm not into processed cheese but plan to try my own unprocessed blend to give it a try. It is 2 parts provolone, 1 part cheddar and 1 part Swiss. It's much easier to go with straight mozzarella, but if you want to experiment...

Chapter 7

THE MEAT

I f I had my choice of just one topping, it would be a good Italian sausage. It's sad to say that most pizzerias have gone to precooked sausage. I'll pass. It's not for me!

In the early days of pizza, there wasn't such a thing as pre-cooked sausage, and life was much better in the pizza world. To me, pre-cooked sausage ranks with the "buttery flavored" soybean oil they put on yellow theater popcorn, out-of-the-box pre-pattied hamburgers served in nearly every restaurant, and the chemically raised dough that in-house bakeries use. I'm old school!

Central Wisconsin had 10 great pizza parlors as I was growing up from my teens into my 30s, but they all disappeared due to deaths or sell outs and were never the same afterwards. I'll never understand that! Each one made its own sausage, and each had its own distinct flavor. Most parlors used whole fennel seed, while others used cracked fennel, ground fennel or anise seed.

Some stores did it all; they ground and seasoned their meat (a few still do) while others had the meat ground at their butcher shops. Most used a mix of pork and beef, but with all my experiments over decades of testing, I find that plain pork is the best, with 10 to 15% fat. My personal favorite is 15%. Butchers use a 3/16-inch "pork plate" and run the meat through only once, which makes a coarse grind.

Ground beef (hamburger) is ground using a smaller 1/8-inch plate and is run through the grinder twice. It mixes better and looks nice when ground twice, but coarsely ground pork has the wonderful "chew" that I want. It also releases from your fingers more easily than a fine grind when applying it to the pizza. Pork butt is my favorite cut of meat for this purpose. Just ask your favorite meat cutter to grind it for you.

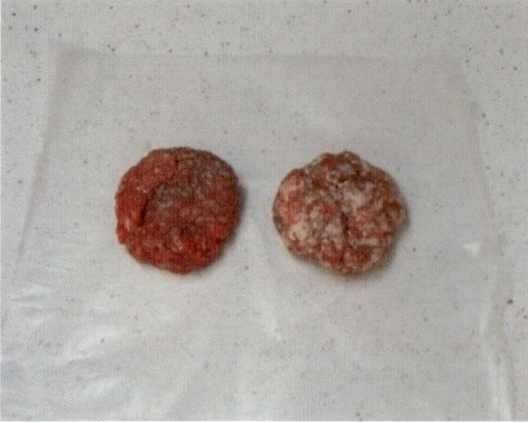

Texture and "chew" are affected by how ground meat is processed. Ground beef, left, was ground twice on a finer grinding plate than the pork on the right, which was ground only once.

If fresh ground pork is already on the shelf but wasn't ground the day you are shopping, I don't recommend buying it. Italian sausage is fussy, and fresh meat is critical. I've even had the meat smell bad when removing it from the wrapping, as though it took on the smell of the material it was packaged in. Instead, I call my meat cutter and ask for 5 1-pound packages, which he freezes right after grinding. I defrost them as needed and add my seasonings.

If buying fresh meat, buy it the day before or the morning you are going to make your pizzas so the seasonings have plenty of time to completely flavor the meat. If you season your meat and then bake pizza without giving the seasonings time to work, it will lack the flavor you want.

Italian sausage formulas for 1 pound pork

This is where a gram scale comes in handy. One pound of sausage should make 3 medium pizzas or 2 extra-large.

Whole fennel seed sausage formula

1 ¾ tsp. salt (10 grams)

¼ tsp. ground black pepper (.42 grams)

1/8 tsp. crushed red pepper flakes (.14 grams) (optional; for a little heat and more for more heat, but increase slowly!)

¼ tsp. granulated garlic (.6 grams, or anywhere up to double the amount for garlic lovers)

½ tsp. whole fennel seed (.7 grams)

Ground fennel seed

For those who don't like biting into a seed.

1 ¾ tsp. salt (10 grams)

¼ tsp. ground black pepper (.42 grams)

1/8 tsp. crushed red pepper flakes (.14 grams) for heat

2 tsp. ground fennel (2.83 grams) It takes a lot!

Cracked fennel or anise seed

1 ¾ tsp. salt (10 grams)

¼ tsp. ground black pepper (.42 grams)

1/8 tsp. crushed red pepper flakes

½ tsp. cracked fennel or anise seed (1.2 grams)

¼ tsp. granulated garlic or double for garlic lovers (.6–1.2 grams)

Break up ground pork in a wide bowl and add ingredients for mixing (right). After seasoning the meat, be sure to keep it tightly wrapped and refrigerated (below).

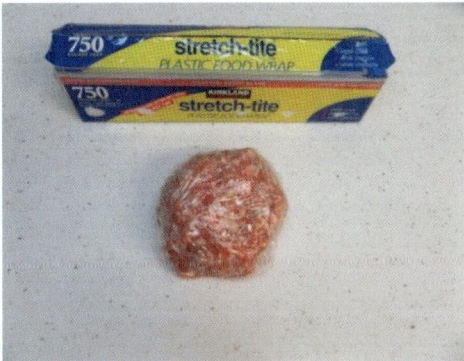

For all formulas, mix spices together with hands just washed with soap and hot water or use food grade gloves. Press sausage out in a large bowl and sprinkle seasoning over the meat. Mix by pulling the meat in from the sides of the dish and pushing down with the fingers. Repeat until ingredients are thoroughly mixed. It takes about a minute. Wrap snuggly in food grade plastic and store in your refrigerator until ready to use. I don't like to freeze seasoned sausage. It loses flavor.

Once seasoned, the meat ages rapidly, and I always want to use it the day after it's seasoned. Sometimes, even then, it's starting to go downhill. It shouldn't be bad; just not as good as it should be. If there is sausage left over from making pizza, I make breakfast sausage with it the following day, although it's a little salty for breakfast. If you want to make the sausage solely for breakfast, cut the salt down to 1 teaspoon.

If you want to go really lean, grind pork tenderloin instead of pork butt. I personally don't care for the "chew." It loses its tenderness and flavor when it's too lean, so I go with 15% fat. If you find grease puddles around your sausage after baking, you probably have about 20% fat, which might be a little too much.

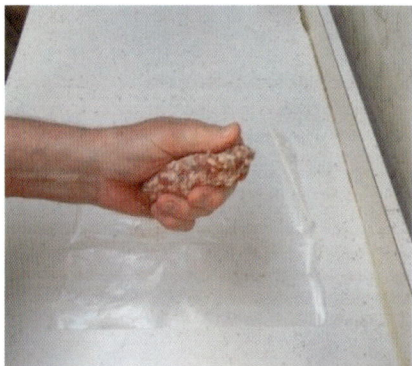

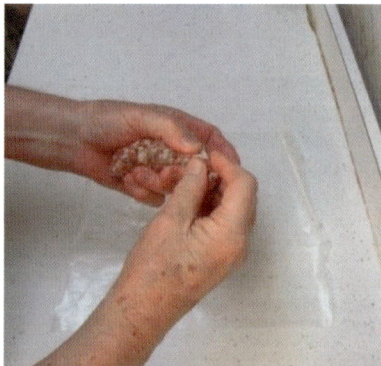

Applying the sausage to the pizza

My favorite technique is to grab a chunk of meat (3 or 4 ounces- worth; not too much) and roll it into a fat link between my palms. I'm right handed so I squeeze the meat in my left hand, drawing the tube of meat out to my thumb, pointer and middle finger. While I'm doing this, I'm grabbing the size pieces I want to apply to my pizza. After a few sausage pizzas, you'll get the hang of it.

Chapter 8

TOPPING YOUR PIZZA

I n the good old days of pizza, the various toppings were quite standard. Now days the modern pizzeria operator has added everything from soup to nuts, as the saying goes. I'm still old school and stick with traditional toppings.

Plain cheese

If my wife and I are traveling, I seek out the best "ma and pa" pizza in a strange town (we never stop at a chain). If they don't use fresh sausage—and most of the time they don't—I'll order a plain cheese. Even then, I often wonder why I stopped. The crust disappoints me, and often so does the sauce, so what's the point? My wife will always ask, so why did you order pizza? My reply is, because I have to!

I've never considered cheese as a topping; it's a base. There is nothing wrong with a plain cheese pizza. As a matter of fact, I like them and encourage everyone to start at home with plain cheese. Make a few small or medium cheese pizzas before adding toppings, just to get used to the art or craft of having the most fun in the kitchen that I know of. Turn your oven on, roll out the dough, ladle on the sauce, add the cheese, bake, cut and serve. There's nothing faster or simpler!

A bubble may appear in the crust from time to time during baking, especially when making a "light" pizza like a plain cheese. The bubble is coming from the yeast in the dough. I like the small ones, but gently pop the larger ones.

Sausage and pepperoni

I've heard that about 1/3 of all pizzas sold are pepperoni pizzas. My thought on that is, if the stores had good Italian sausage, there would be fewer pepperoni eaters.

Pepperoni first started showing up in New York pizzerias near the end of WWI. It is pork and beef mixed with spicy peppers like paprika in a sausage casing. It is dried and cured. The end result is a spicy, smoky flavor and bright red color. Pepperoni is similar to Italian salami, but its texture is soft and more finely ground than salami. Pepperoni can be purchased as a stick but is most often pre-sliced, packaged and sold in the sandwich meat aisle of a grocery story. You can also find pepperoni made with turkey meat.

A medium pepperoni pizza sliced in squares makes a nice presentation at the table.

On a pizza, the edges of pepperoni may curl and leave grease pockets when baked. That can be controlled by putting the pepperoni under the cheese. If the grease bothers you in the pepperoni, go with Hormel's turkey, which leaves no grease.

Plain Sausage without a lot of other toppings is still my favorite pizza. I like pepperoni, but not combined with sausage where the pepperoni tends to dominate. Generally I like my meat on top of the cheese, but if I'm making a sausage and pepperoni, I will put the pepperoni under the cheese so I'm not slicing it in half or chasing it all over the pizza when I cut it. It just looks nicer.

So, what's the difference between plain sausage and Italian sausage?

Back in the 1970s when I loved Pizza Hut (before they were bought out), they had both pizzas on the menu. If you ordered a plain sausage pizza, you got pre-cooked hamburger, but if you ordered Italian sausage, you got the real deal. It was made from bulk pork with fennel seed. Yum!

Pieces of sausage lay neatly across sliced mozzarella on this unbaked pizza. It was prepared in a cutter pan and shows excess dough removed.

Italian sausage is ground pork with garlic and fennel, and sometimes red pepper flakes to warm it up. Another type of sausage, breakfast sausage, is ground pork with black pepper and ground sage as the main spices.

My favorite pizza parlor of all time does not have the delicious sausage they once had before the owner died, but it's still better than the chains' and everyone else's precooked meat. Surprisingly, even with the huge difference and loss in flavor from earlier days, their number-one seller is still a plain sausage pizza. Mmmm.

Veggie pizza

Canned or fresh mushrooms, onion, green pepper, black and green olives are all the old traditional toppings, but today, pretty much anything goes. Whatever fits you and your family, go for it. The main thing is, go easy. Less is better; otherwise you end up with a casserole, and pizzas don't bake out well when loaded up.

My opinion is, no pizza should have more than 5 toppings, but sometimes I have to make a rule breaker. Our son-in-law enjoys about 5 meats and all the veggies, so I do it just for him, but I go easy on the quantities. On a thin crust pizza, I put the veggies under the cheese and sausage or pepperoni on top.

Shrimp pizza

Shrimp pizza is certainly not as popular as the others, but for those of you who like shrimp on a pizza, I can tell you how to make the best.

Drain a can of small deveined shrimp, then sauce your dough as usual and top with the shrimp. If you prefer raw or frozen shrimp, you will want to precook them. Add whatever else you might like for a topping, but don't go nuts. A friend of ours likes black olives with shrimp. Just plain shrimp is probably the best choice. One nice addition is a light drizzle of shrimp sauce over the top before baking. It really enhances the shrimp pizza.

Chicken

Cooked chicken, cut pieces of broccoli and onion on a white ranch sauce produce a nice pizza. I like to squeeze a couple cloves of fresh garlic into this sauce, then spread it on the dough with my fingers. It doesn't like to spread too easily with a ladle, although a nice flat spoon might work. Try them all, but fingers work great!

There is a recipe for the white sauce in chapter 5.

Apply the sauce, and then add chunks of cooked chicken, onion (if you want it), and then the cheese on last.

The margherita pizza

Margherita means "daisy" in Italian. Some say this pizza was made in honor of the queen of Italy, but others say the pizza was popular in Naples long before that particular queen was even born. You can research it if you like. One thing is for sure, the primary colors of the pizza's ingredients—sauce, basil and mozzarella—are the same red, green and white as on the national flag of Italy.

A margherita pizza before baking highlights traditional red, green and white colors of the Italian flag. This one was rolled and then laid on a wooden peel where the toppings were added. It will be baked on a stone or steel surface.

The best sauce for this specialty pizza calls for San Marzano tomatoes. Drain the liquid from canned San Marzanos and squeeze them until they break into pieces. Watch out. They squirt! If you don't care to mess with the San Marzanos, use whatever sauce you prefer. Crushed tomato would still be my choice.

I like squeezing a couple of large cloves of garlic into this sauce and holding the salt off until last. Roll out your dough and apply the tomato sauce, lay fresh basil leaves sunny-side up on the sauce (it doesn't take a lot of them), then place a big chunk of fresh mozzarella on each leaf. If you don't care to buy fresh mozzarella, just use your aged cheese, but this is where the fresh works really well.

Sprinkle kosher salt lightly over the top, bake, cut and serve with a drizzle of mild olive oil on each piece per individual taste. Most pizza shops will drizzle the oil on before baking. I add afterwards. It's a taste preference, and not everyone wants the oil.

This is a very bland pizza if using fresh mozzarella, so you might want to add some extra salt to the sauce.

The tasty feta pizza
Although this is a meatless pizza, it's a favorite for most pizza lovers we have over to our house.

Before baking, this Detroit style deep dish pizza is topped with onion, mushroom, mozzarella, black olives, diced tomato and feta cheese.

This is another pizza where I like to squeeze 2 or 3 cloves of fresh garlic in the sauce. For a round pizza, apply sauce to the middle of the rolled dough and spread it out almost to the edge. For a square pan, apply sauce in strips lengthwise. Top with onion and mushrooms, followed by mozzarella cheese. On top, I add black olives, diced tomato and the delicious feta cheese, diced into small pieces.

There are basically two types of feta; cow's milk and goat's milk. We prefer the cow's, but try them both. Bake at 500 degrees for approximately 10 minutes, cut and serve. Offer an olive oil drizzle for those who want it.

Taco pizza

For a totally different, but delicious pizza, this one does the trick. It starts with a different sauce, which is a mixture of picante sauce and crushed tomato or puree. The recipe is in chapter 5, but there is a caution that bears repeating. My favorite taco sauce is Pace Picante. Their hot sauce is really hot, so be careful if you go that route.

We don't use raw sausage here; we pre-cook lean ground beef and add taco seasonings. The first time I made this, I bought a packet of powdered taco seasoning and didn't care for it. It didn't have enough flavor, so I started making my own.

Taco spice for 1 pound ground beef
1 1/8 tsp. salt (6.4 gr).
2 tsp. chili powder (5.0 gr).
1 tsp. ground cumin (1.8 gr).
¼ tsp. black pepper (.56 gr).
¼ tsp. Cayenne pepper (.56 gr).
¼ scant tsp. granulated garlic (.56 gr).
¼ tsp. fennel seed (.6 gr) (It's not typically Mexican, but I like it)

Brown the ground beef, drain and stir in the seasonings. Cool slightly, and it's ready to add to your taco pizza.

For a thin crust, roll dough out an inch wider than the pan you are using and lay it over the pan. For square pan or deep dish, follow the dough instructions in chapter 4. Apply sauce, sprinkle on the flavored cooked beef, add diced onion, jalapeños (optional), and then cheese. This is where a little mild cheddar mix is good, or an 80-10-10 blend (mozzarella, provolone, cheddar). Top with black olives and diced tomatoes. Bake at 500 to 550 degrees for approximately 10 minutes until the crust is golden brown.

Serve with crisp shredded lettuce on top and sour cream on the side. I have seen stores add the lettuce first and then bake. Ugh! I like to add it after baking so it isn't soggy and wilted. For tasty sour cream, add chives or one teaspoon of Lawry's Seasoned Salt to 8 ounces sour cream. Lawry's does not contain monosodium glutamate.

Anchovy pizza

I better hit on the controversial pizza, the anchovy pizza. Whenever we have a gang over for pizza, I will always ask what they would like on their pizza. The answers are always the same; anything but ancho-vies! On the other hand, I have a relative who is a full blooded Italian, and she can't get enough of the salty little fish.

For those who say they aren't crazy about anchovies, I break the fish into small pieces and don't put much on the pizza. That way they can at least see what the anchovy is all about. They might not ask for it again, but they have at least tried it. My wife and I do like an occasional anchovy and onion pizza, but again, not going heavy on the fish.

Hawaiian pizza

Although many like this ham and pineapple pizza, if I had a pizza parlor, you would not see it on the menu. I do not put pineapple on pizza! I think Dole came up with the Hawaiian pizza recipe to sell more pineapple. If I were making it (and this is a big "if"), I would use Canadian bacon instead of ham.

Chapter 9

VARIOUS STYLES OF PIZZA AND ASSEMBLY

After years of experimentation, I have come up with a set of simple ingredients, simple formulas and simple steps to make great pizza. You may find that after doing your own experimenting your favorite pizza is a little different from mine, but it pays to start with a solid foundation. Following are the amounts that I use.

If pan baking, I highly recommend using the pans I have researched from LloydPans to get the most out of your home pizza making experience. The aluminum serving trays sold at retail stores are not designed for baking and won't give you the golden brown, crispy crusts you want. LloydPans also have design elements that make assembly and clean-up much easier.

Step-by-step assembly directions are below, followed by a quick reference to guide you through the quantities of dough, sauce and cheese for each style. Another quick reference—by pizza size—is in Appendix B, "Measurements for Dough."

Thin Crust, Pan Baking

Providing you have the cutter pans from LloydPans, when making a thin crust pizza, roll your dough out a good inch wider than the cutter pan (explanation coming up). Using my recommended dough weights from Chapter 4, two inches wider makes for a thinner crust, whereas a half inch wider makes a thicker crust.

You can use the pan as is or spray it with oil. I prefer to sprinkle it with cornmeal. The results resemble a hearth baked pizza. Place the rolled dough over the pan. Working your way around the outside of the pan, lift the edges of the dough and lightly push the dough into the inside corners of the pan. If you fail to do this, the dough will pull away from the pan and shrink while baking. We don't want shrinkage. I let the excess dough hang over the pan until all the toppings are added. This prevents getting any food between the dough and the pan.

When starting out, I strongly recommend making several small or medium size pizzas to get used to rolling out the dough, and make just plain cheese pizzas for practice. Plain cheese pizzas are really pretty good! Once you feel comfortable working with the dough, then and only then, move up to the larger sizes, if you need them. It won't be difficult if you start out small.

How the cutter pan works

A cutter pan's top edge is sharp enough that when running a rolling pin over the dough, it cuts it, trimming the excess dough off. Once the pizza is assembled, using your dough cutter rolling pin, trim the excess dough and lift the pan away from the trimmings (rather than the trimmings away from the pan). A full size rolling pin will work for cutting, as long as your toppings aren't so high that the roller hits them.

When a small rolling pin is rolled over a cutter pan, its sharp edge "cuts" away excess dough. Add toppings before cutting, and lift the pan up and away from the trim, rather than trim away from the pan.

Save all your dough trimmings in a food storage bag in the refrigerator. If your trimmings each weigh 3 ounces as mine do, after three pizzas you should have enough trimmings for another medium crust. Trimmings from four pizzas will make an extra-large. Once the trimmings have been together in the refrigerator for a day, they are ready to be rounded up into another dough ball for future use.

Pre-heat your oven as hot as it will go (500 to 550 degrees). Unlike frozen pizza, fresh dough pizza loves heat. Wood and coal-fired ovens run 800 to 900 degrees and bake pizzas in about 90 seconds, so don't worry about burning your pizza at the low setting of 500 or 550. When using pizza pans, you don't need to pre-heat the oven for an hour as so many stone bakers do. As soon as your oven is up to temperature, place your pizza pan on the center rack and bake for 7 to 10 minutes. Plain cheese takes less time; more toppings take more time.

Ovens vary, so it will take a few bakings to learn your oven temperatures and times. I've seen ovens 100 degrees off to the low side, and after 10 minutes of baking, the pizza was barely bubbling.

If your crust isn't coming out brown and crispy like it should, use a pan gripper or oven mitt to move the pizza from the center rack to the bottom rack for a couple minutes for added browning. Hopefully your oven will run hot and it won't be necessary.

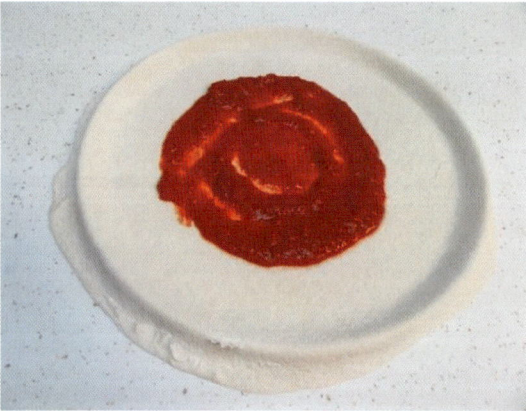

Here is a tip for spreading sauce in a cutter pan. Pour a ladleful in the center of the dough and gently spread it out in a spiral using the bottom of the ladle. Thicker sauces like white sauce often spread better with clean fingers. Add toppings before trimming away the excess dough.

Stone baking with no pan

Outdoor wood-fired brick pizza ovens are becoming increasingly popular where one can bake at much higher temperatures, but the average home pizza maker just bakes on a stone in the kitchen oven. Stones can crack, but there are also steel plates to bake on that might be a better deal. When using a stone or steel baking surface, give them time to preheat before baking the pizza. If you stone bake, I also suggest you invest in both a wood and a metal peel. Each has a specific use (see Chapter 3).

Since there are no pans or trimmings to deal with, just roll the dough out to the desired size. No trimming also means you can use smaller (less weight) dough balls.

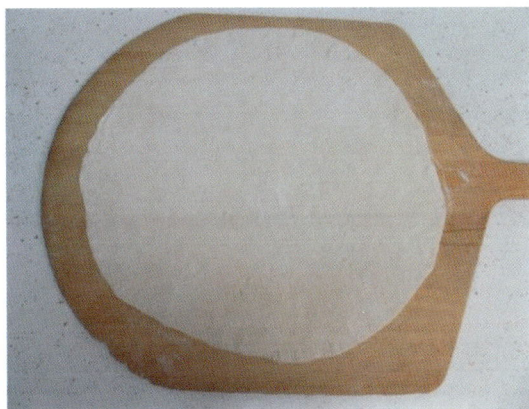

Add topping ingredients quickly once your dough is on the wood peel so it doesn't get sticky. A light dusting of flour on the peel will help your dough circle slide off more easily.

Place the rolled dough on a wood peel, lay on the toppings as quickly as possible and immediately slide the pizza onto the hot stone. If the pizza sits on the peel too long, it can sweat and stick. When you try to slide it off the peel and into the oven, the toppings will slide off, but the dough will remain, and you will have a smoke alarm mess! Handling a peel requires a bit of finesse, so many pizza recipes call for sprinkling corn meal on the peel to act as rollers, making the pizza slide easier. I don't recommend it. Corn meal will burn on the stone if not swept off after each baking. That's messy. I prefer using a light dusting of semolina flour instead.

Before sliding a pizza into the oven, make absolutely certain it is free of the peel. This is where the finesse comes in. Use a few rapid, short sideways jiggles to loosen the pizza from the wood peel and then quickly jerk the peel out from under the dough to slide it into the stone. It takes practice. If the dough doesn't break loose when you jiggle it, it isn't going to slide off when you attempt to place it on the stone. Unlike pan baking, you have just one shot at placing the pizza in the right spot. This is especially important when making a 15-inch pizza and sliding it onto a

15-inch stone. I strongly suggest making smaller pizzas until you become seasoned at this critical stage of the art.

Bake times will vary from one oven to the next. Test for doneness by lifting the outside edge of the crust with a metal peel after 5 or 6 minutes. The pizza is done when the crust is a nice golden brown and sauce is bleeding through a creamy white cheese. If the pizza needs more time, you can use the metal peel and your fingers to turn it a quarter or half turn on the stone to bake for another few minutes. Professional pizza makers are always rotating their pizzas to insure more even browning.

Remove the finished pizza with a metal peel and slide it onto a cardboard circle or serving tray. What you don't want to do is place a hot pizza on a cold tray, which ends in a soggy crust. Either warm the tray first or put a piece of parchment paper on the tray before the pizza gets there. Cut and serve.

Chicago style deep dish
Oil the bottom and sides of a round 2-inch deep pan with your choice of oil. Roll out the dough so that when placing it in the pan, it covers the bottom and all the way up the sides. Test that out before oiling the pan to get the right size. Press and "flute" the dough around the edges of the pan so the walls of the pizza are thinner than the bottom.

Cover and place in a warm spot to allow the dough to rise. Heat kills yeast, so it has to have time to work on the dough before it goes in the oven. This step makes for a much nicer, lighter crust but may take a couple of hours in a warm place, so a little planning ahead is in order.

Once the dough has risen in the pan, place it uncovered in a pre-heated 300-degree oven for 5 minutes to "set" the dough. Once that is done, toppings can be assembled anytime.

Deep-dish pizzas are called "upside down" pizzas. The toppings go in first, then the cheese, followed by the sauce last. The main advantage to this is that the cheese can never burn. Chicago pizzerias don't pre-bake their dough, because they feel it rises as it bakes under the toppings. True, their dough rises quickly in the oven—I suspect they use leavening agents—but it can never be as light as ours.

Those pizza makers also put the raw patty of sausage in first (if it's a sausage pizza, of course), followed by the other toppings. Next comes cheese and a generous

This beautiful Chicago style deep dish pizza is built upside-down, with toppings and cheese going in the pan before a layer of rich crushed tomato.

portion of a crushed tomato-type sauce. If using raw sausage, I recommend making it into chunks and putting it on top where the heat can hit it.

Place your pizza pan on the center rack of a preheated 500-degree oven and bake approximately 10 minutes. Remove with the deep dish pan grippers or mitt when the crust is a golden brown. Allow your pizza to rest a few minutes, then remove it from the pan with a spatula and place on a cardboard circle or serving tray topped with a parchment paper sweat barrier. Cut into wedges.

In a commercial kitchen, the pizza is removed from the pan, cut, and slid back in the pan to keep it hot. It's up to you, but you might find that can be a bit messy.

Detroit style deep dish
This style uses a square pan and is my favorite when going deep!

I have relatives in Detroit, so I was introduced to Detroit's pizza years ago. The first time we ate it, it didn't do much for me, and I was trying to figure out how they made it. Well, once I ordered the square pans and made my own, it was a big, wow! Most pizzerias have two or more dough formulas for the different styles of pizza they make. At home, my one simple dough formula works so well in both thick and thin, why not leave it alone?

To make your own Detroit style, lightly oil the square pan bottom and half way up the sides. Roll the dough a little larger than the bottom of the pan. Then, placing it in the pan, pull in the sides to fit the pan. This works better than rolling it too small and trying to stretch it out. If your dough is too small and doesn't fit corner to corner, you will have to keep pressing it out to fill the pan, which is more work, plus it tends to shrink away from the sides. If you get shrinkage, let the dough rest 10 minutes or so, and then press it out to fit the pan. Once it is fully proofed, don't try any more adjustments. You'll just deflate the dough.

Cover the pan and allow the dough to rise until doubled in size, and then place it uncovered in a pre-heated 300-degree oven for 5 minutes to set the dough. Once this is done, you can add the toppings and bake anytime up to a couple of days later. For instance, do the pre-bake the night before or the morning of, then after cooling, simply keep covered until ready to assemble and bake. (You don't have to par-bake the crust. You can just let the dough rise, add your toppings and bake. Just be very careful not to bump the pan, which will knock down [deflate] the dough.)

Mozzarella is spread all the way to the edge of the pan for this small Detroit style deep dish pizza so that it comes out with a crisp fringe of caramelized cheese. Romano was shredded over the top after baking.

To assemble, layer on the toppings and then cover the dough with cheese all the way to the edges of the pan. That's a big part of this pizza. As it bakes, the cheese runs over the edge and caramelizes. That's like frosting on a cake. Awesome!

We like to ladle the sauce on top of the cheese lengthwise in strips; a small pan with two strips, large pan with 3 strips. We don't flood the square pan like the round. I believe some Detroiters add the sauce after baking. See which you like better, but I prefer adding before baking. As with other pizzas, if you are using raw sausage, I recommend you put it on top so it gets thoroughly cooked.

Detroit pizza makers use brick cheese or brick with half white cheddar, but I don't see a gain when using it. Some use aged and others mild brick. Brick is a Wisconsin cheese and is very similar to mozzarella when young. It gets nuttier and more pungent as it ages, but it doesn't string out like mozzarella. Try it if you like, but a quality mozzarella works just fine for me. I always portion my cheese to fit the crust, with a thin crust getting not much cheese and a thick crust getting more cheese, keeping things in proper proportion. Pizzas are all about balance.

Place the pan on the center rack of a preheated 500-degree oven and bake approximately 10 minutes. Remove with an oven mitt (don't use pan grippers with the square pan) when the crust is golden brown.

Just like any pizza, light brown will give you a softer crust, and dark brown will mean a harder crust. The flavor also changes as the crust gets darker. I like a medium golden brown. You will know the color you like after a few bakes.

Pan style

The only differences between a deep dish (Chicago style) and pan style is that we don't bring the dough up the sides in pan style, and the sauce and cheese stop short of the edges.

Pizza Hut has the handle on pan style and sells millions of them. They proof the dough in proofer ovens and allow the dough to rise quickly. Although they might taste good, I think they go heavy on seasoned oil, and they look kind of deep fried. I haven't eaten one in decades. At home, we can produce an excellent pan style with just a small amount of olive oil in the deep dish pan.

Lightly oil the bottom of a deep dish pan, roll dough to fit (9-ounce ball for a small and 13-ounce for a large), place the dough in the pan, cover, allow to rise until double in a warm place, then bake uncovered in a preheated 300-degree oven for 5 minutes to set the crust.

Gently spread the sauce, cheese and toppings, stopping just short of the edge. Place the pan on the center rack of a preheated 500-degree oven and bake approximately 10 minutes or until the crust is golden brown.

If you choose not to par-bake the dough, be gentle while layering on the toppings and getting the pan into the oven so you don't knock the dough down. It's tricky, but it can be done.

Garlic strips

This has to be the tastiest treat!

You've had pizza fries right? Well, these are my answer to store-bought frozen pizza fries that come on commercial cracker crusts full of chemicals, preservatives and some kind of garlic flavored oil. My recipe uses unadulterated dough and real garlic.

Roll dough (9-ounce ball for a small, 13-ounce for a large), place in a lightly oiled 1.5-inch-deep pan and brush with garlic butter (see recipe below). Top with cheese almost to the edge of the pan. I love to add jalapeños. If you're not so sure, just add to part of the topping, but at least try it!

An oiled pan gives homemade garlic strips a crispy char on the bottom and edges. Try jalapeños on half if not everyone likes the extra heat.

Cover the pan and allow dough to rise in a warm place to double. Bake uncovered on the center rack of a preheated 500-degree oven for approximately 10 minutes. Remove with deep dish pan grippers or oven mitt when the crust is golden brown. Run a spatula around the edge to break the crust loose from the pan. Slip a spatula under one side and slide the crust onto a serving tray and cut in strips. It you don't spread cheese quite all the way to the edge, it will make removal a little easier.

I never wash my garlic strip pan. Just wipe it clean with soft paper toweling, like cleaning cast iron frying pans.

Garlic butter formula
1 stick salted butter
2-4 cloves fresh garlic (more is better)
2 tsp. salt

Lightly melt the butter, add salt, squeeze in garlic and stir.

If you don't have a garlic press, you will find that a good quality one is a tool you'll learn to love. I bought a cheap model years ago and the handles bent. I prefer Cutco or Pampered Chef, but there are a lot of choices out there. A garlic peeler also makes life easier.

If salt is an issue, start with 1 teaspoon and add more until you find what's right for you. If you use this formula for garlic toast—rather than on a pizza crust—skip the salt altogether.

Thoughts on cutting a pizza
Sure, it is sometimes called a pizza pie, but that doesn't mean a pizza should be cut like a pie. I like squares for practical reasons.

If you cut an extra-large pizza in pie wedges, you get pretty big pieces. That's fine if you are a New York pizza maker and selling by the slice. Who would want to pay $3 for a small piece? But that is also why New Yorkers have to fold their slice in order to eat it. That's not how I want to eat pizza. I want no fork and no fold.

On the other hand, if you cut it in squares, they stay pretty much uniform no matter what size pizza you're serving. I also like the looks of a pizza with one pepperoni or one sausage on each square. I get a lot of compliments on presentation. Just look at the photos!

When I cut mine, I have 12 pieces to a small, 21 to a medium and 32 for large (14-inch) or extra-large (over 14-inch). The pieces are pretty much uniform in size and easy to eat.

A quick reference for quantities of dough, sauce and cheese

Thin crust with a cutter pan
Dough
When pan baking, use a 5-ounce dough ball for a small pizza, a 9-ounce for a medium and 13-ounce for a large or extra-large.

Sauce

Use a 2- or 3-ounce ladle.

For a small (9"), use 2-3 ounces

For a medium (12"), 4-5 ounces

For a large (14"), 6-7 ounces

For an extra-large (15"), use 7-8 ounces

Cheese

I prefer lighter amounts on thin crusts.

For a small use 2-3 ounces

For a medium use 4-6 ounces

For a large use 6-7 ounces

For an extra-large use 8-10 ounces

Square pan

Dough

For the 8 x 10" use 8-10 ounce balls

For the 10 x 14" use 13-18 ounces

Start out using a 9-ounce ball for the 8 x 10" and 13-ounce for the 10 x 14".

I recommend using these amounts the first time you make this delicious treat. If you desire a thinner crust, knock it down a little, and if you want thicker, add a little more, but only one ounce at a time.

Cheese

For the 8 x 10" use 6-8 ounces

For the 10 x 14" use 11-14 ounces

Sauce (apply last)

For an 8 x 10" ladle two strips of sauce lengthwise, but stay in from the sides a little. It takes about two ounces per strip.

For a 10 x 14" ladle three strips of sauce lengthwise and about 3 ounces per strip.

This is where I prefer using crushed tomato and lightly sprinkling Greek oregano over the top before baking.

Deep dish

Dough

For the small (9"), use 10-12 ounces dough

For the large (12"), use 17-21 ounces dough

Cheese

For the small, use 8-10 ounces cheese

For the large, use 14-18 ounces cheese

Sauce

This is an "upside down" pizza, so apply the sauce last.

For the small use 5-6 ounces sauce (crushed tomato).

For the large use 8-10 ounces sauce (crushed tomato).

I sprinkle oregano over the sauce on this one also and sprinkle with grated hard cheese after baking.

Chapter 10

REHEATING LEFTOVER PIZZA

When we finish a pizza party at our home, there are usually no leftovers, but that isn't saying there couldn't be. Whether there are just a couple pieces or more, how are you going to handle the leftovers and how are you going to reheat them?

Store leftovers in a plastic food storage bag or other sealed container in the refrigerator. Some like to eat pizza cold, but if you don't have anything that will spoil, like sausage, it can be left on the counter to eat at room temperature.

If you like it hot, there are a few reheating methods folks use, but they can have some drawbacks. You can preheat the kitchen oven to 400 degrees and place leftovers on a pan for 10 minutes or so, but it will dry out your leftovers.

Reheating in a countertop pizza oven is another option that, when carefully done and not over-heated, works pretty well. However, the cheese can run over the edges if not careful. Placing the pizza on aluminum foil would help with that. Be careful that the foil doesn't contact the heating elements.

For quick and easy, many will use their microwave, which definitely heats it up but also softens the crust, which I don't like at all. I have never done it and never will.

Ranking number 1 on the reheat-leftovers scale is my recommended technique. Put a single-layer of your leftovers in an unoiled pan and put the cover on. Start at medium heat for 5 minutes or so, and then reduce to medium-low.

It should take 10 to 15 minutes for the first batch. Slide those pieces onto a plate and turn the heat down a little more for the subsequent batches. They won't take as long. You can only get so many pieces in a large frying pan, but the results are well worth it!

This works better than any other method for keeping the crust crisp while heating through. I like having the cheese run off a little and get crispy brown in the pan, but if the heat is too high it will burn. A little lower heat and more time works best.

With this reheat method, your pizza will turn out almost as good as the first bake.

Chapter 11

IN A PINCH—DOCTORING A FROZEN PIZZA

When you don't have time, are not prepared to make a fresh pizza from scratch, or don't want to spend $20 or more for a run-of-the-mill retail pizza, there is an alternative. Buy a cheap frozen one, and do your own doctoring. With my recommendations and your topping choices, this pizza-of-last-resort can come out tasting pretty good.

Premium frozen pizzas can run $6 to $11 and don't give you any advantage over the economy brands—those I refer to as babysitter pizzas—when it comes to doctoring. The economy brands are often on sale for four for $10, three for $9 and sometimes five for $10.

A counter-top pizza oven is ideal for this job, but if you don't have one, use your kitchen oven and preheat it to 450 degrees (or by trial and error to a temperature that works best for you).

No matter what the base you start with—plain cheese, sausage, or sausage and pepperoni—add any extra toppings you want to the frozen pizza, but don't add the extra mozzarella yet. If you add cheese right away, it will brown too fast, and you will have to remove the pizza from the oven before the crust is done.

Bake the doctored pizza for about ten minutes or until the cheese starts to brown. Pull it from the oven and sprinkle a handful or two of additional mozzarella over the top. Extend the cheese to within 1/2-inch of the edge. You don't want to leave a big dry edge.

Return the pizza to the oven and bake until the crust is how you want it to be, nice and brown.

This two-step baking is the only way I have found to get the crust brown without destroying the top. The friends I have shared this technique with love it.

Enjoy!

Chapter 12

JOIN THE CLUB

Ihave given you as much information as I can in written form and all in layman's terms, making it possible for the home pizza baker to understand how fast, simple and easy it really is to make pizza. Once you've been making pizzas for a while, I'd appreciate you making a review on Amazon and tell others what you think.

Although this small book covers quite well the topic of baking pizzas in your kitchen oven, there is more information available at my website. It contains dozens of descriptive videos giving you more information in detail and showing how to do each step. As they say, a picture video is worth a thousand words.

Although there are tons of free YouTube videos from individuals sharing their concoctions, I don't believe there's another site like mine or any YouTubers who can give you the knowledge you will gain from my teachings. What I share with you is not some homespun philosophy, but rather, the information you need, all learned from many years of studying the professionals and experimenting.

With my close-up videos, I show you all the things we talk about in detail, taking all the mystery out of each step and making the art of homemade pizza simple.

Should you desire to go deeper with this great passion, it's a one-time fee of $14.95 to join the Pizza Club of America. Book buyers even get a $5 discount on membership. We'd love to have you!

https://www.homepizzaparlor.com/book-reader-login/

POSTSCRIPT

SCHNAPPS THE PIZZA DOG

Pizza tends to be a family affair with everyone under your roof getting in on the act. At one time, our family included a schnauzer named Schnapps.

It was during one of our evening pizza parties, when he was about two that he became interested in pizza and stood by watching me remove the pizzas from our pizza oven. After the last pizza came out for the gang, he let out a little yip, so I made a cheese pizza and cut it into smaller squares. When it was cool, I tossed pieces to Schnapps, which he caught like a pro, never missing a piece. He ate half of a 12-inch pizza, and the other half remained on the counter.

Schnapps never had to go out during the night, so I was surprised when he woke me up several hours later. I followed him to the kitchen where he stood under the counter looking up at his pizza. He wanted more!

From that night on, I called him our pizza dog and made a special medium cheese pizza for him every time I baked. The funny thing is, when I would serve someone else's fresh pizza (frozen was never an option) he would turn it down.

We had Schnapps, for 15 years. He never ate dog food and was never sick, but I believe during those 15 years he ate more pizza than most humans!

Our schnauzer, Schnapps, developed a serious love of pizzas as a 2-year-old and probably ate more pizza than most humans during his 15-year life span. This is Schnapps with my wife, Sherry.

Appendix A

RESOURCES

Pan and Equipment Dealers
http://lloydpans.com/home-pizza-parlor (my page where you can use promo code 10HPP to get a discount on your purchases)

https://www.northenpizzaequipment.com

Cheese
www.vernscheese.com/retail-store/

https://www.burnettdairy.com

Sauces
www.amazon.com and search for Stanislaus Full-Red. (Stanislaus has its own website but does not sell directly to consumers.)

Spices
https://www.zanehellas.com/shop/ (The company makes a number of oregano essential oils, but the dried herb is available on their website for culinary use too.)

www.amazon.com (another source for Zane Hellas Oregano)

MEASUREMENTS FOR DOUGH, SAUCE AND CHEESE BY PIZZA SIZE

SMALL 9" THIN CRUST

5 ounces dough
2 ounces sauce
2 ounces cheese

MEDIUM 12" THIN CRUST

9 ounces dough
4 ounces sauce
4 ounces cheese

LARGE 14" THIN CRUST

13 ounces dough (12 would work but everything we
weigh out is 9 or 13, so it's just one more ounce to trim)
6 ounces sauce
6 ounces cheese

EXTRA LARGE 15" THIN CRUST

13 ounces dough
8 ounces sauce
8 ounces cheese

8 x 10" SQUARE PAN

9 ounces dough
6 ounces cheese
4 ounces sauce (2strips lengthwise)

10 x 14" SQUARE PAN

13 ounces dough
11 ounces cheese
9 ounces sauce (3 strips lengthwise)

SMALL 9" DEEP DISH

10-11 ounces dough
8 ounces cheese
5 ounces sauce (crushed tomato preferred)

LARGE 12" DEEP DISH

17-18 ounces dough
14 ounces cheese
8 ounces sauce (crushed tomato preferred)

COST COMPARISON CHART

These prices came from a real menu at a very popular Wisconsin pizza parlor. Keep in mind that a 15-inch pizza made at home is 13% more pizza than a 14-inch "large" at a pizza parlor.

Comparing costs for a family of four

Dining at home 15" thin crust- 5 toppings		Dining at a pizza parlor 14" thin crust- 5 toppings	
All pizza ingredients	$6.00	One Combo Pizza	$23.35
Husband's two beers	$2.00	Husband's two beers	$6.50
Wife's glass of wine	$2.00	Wife's glass of wine	$5.00
Kid's 2 sodas each	$1.00	Kids' 2 sodas each	$4.00
Subtotal	$11.00	Subtotal	$38.85
NO Sales Tax	$0	Sales Tax	$2.15
NO Tip	$0	Tip (approx. 15%)	$6.00
Total	$11.00	Total	$47.00

Printed in Great Britain
by Amazon